Leading People

Expert Solutions to Everyday Challenges

Harvard Business Scnool Publishing

Boston, Massachusetts

Printed in the United States of America

10 09 08 07 06   5 4 3 2 1

Library of Congress Cataloging-in-Publication Data

Pocket mentor. Leading people.
    p. cm. — (Pocket mentor series)
  Includes bibliographical references.
  ISBN 1-4221-0349-8

The paper used in this publication meets the requirements of the American National Standard for Permanence of Paper for Publications and Documents in Libraries and Archives Z39.48-1992

Leading People

Pocket Mentor Series

The books in this series offer immediate solutions to the challenges managers face every day. Each book is packed with handy tools, checklists, and real-life examples, including a Test Yourself section to help identify strengths and weaknesses. For all readers eager to address the daily demands of work, these books are ideal.

Books in the series:

Leading Teams
Running Meetings
Managing Time
Managing Projects
Coaching People
Giving Feedback
Leading People

Contents

Tips and Tools   51

Tools for Leading People   53

Worksheets to help you plan your role as a leader.

Test Yourself   63

A helpful review of concepts presented in this guide. Take the test before and after you've read through the guide to see how much you've learned.

Answers to test questions   66

To Learn More   69

Additional titles of articles and books if you want to go more deeply into the topic.

Sources for Leading People   85

Notes   87

For you to use as ideas come to mind.

Mentor's Message: Leading Starts with Knowing Where and Why You're Going

The word *leader* evokes images of great men and women who, in moments of crisis, rise up to make a great difference in the course of human events. We enjoy books about them, we watch movies about them, and we tell stories about them. Unfortunately, this image creates the belief that in order to lead we somehow have to be at that golden moment and have the ability to inspire thousands. Not so. Leading, simply defined, is the ability to influence others to move toward the accomplishment of common goals. Mothers and fathers lead. Little children lead. Unit heads lead. And you can lead. In fact, you probably already do. Think about the times recently when you have influenced others by the decisions you made, by how you choose to spend your time and money, or by simply engaging in a conversation that affected what others were doing. Our purpose with this guide is not to show you how to lead, but to provide concepts and ideas so that you can do it better.

So where can you start? Start with the purpose. It does very little good to spend time trying to influence others if you have no idea for what purpose. What is the vision? Where are you trying to go? What are you trying to accomplish? This sounds so simple, but it is absolutely critical. Good leaders know what they are trying to accomplish. Not only do they know where they are going but why they are going there. If you cannot answer these questions—where are you going and why—you will spend a lot of time rushing to and fro but getting nowhere. Remember the classic scene from Lewis Carroll's *Alice and Wonderland*?

> *[Alice] was a little startled by seeing the Cheshire Cat sitting on a bough of a tree a few yards off.*
>
> *The Cat only grinned when it saw Alice....*
>
> *"Cheshire Puss," she began, rather timidly,... "Would you tell me, please, which way I ought to go from here?"*
>
> *"That depends a good deal on where you want to get to," said the Cat.*
>
> *"I don't much care where—" said Alice.*
>
> *"Then it doesn't matter which way you go," said the Cat.*
>
> *"—so long as I get somewhere," Alice added as an explanation.*
>
> *"Oh, you're sure to do that," said the Cat, "if you only walk long enough."*

The Cheshire Cat is right. If you do not know where you are going, any path will do. But once you do know where you are headed, then you can focus your resources and motivate and inspire people to get the work done. Remember, if you are going to be a leader, it is not about what you do, it is about what others do. As a leader, you influence others to help you accomplish the common objective.

One last word of caution. Don't wait for others to clarify your vision. In our work in organizations, we are forever hearing the comment, "If only they would tell me where we are going, I would know what to do." That simply tells us the speaker is not a leader; he's a follower waiting for someone else to lead. And guess what! You already know more about your job, your life, your customers, your hopes and desires than "they" do. Why are you waiting for them? Leaders do not wait.

I hope this guide will be useful, helping you to take the risk and be the leader you already are. Often all you have to do is step out and say to yourself, "Okay, I am in charge and I know where I want to go." Then say to others, "Follow me."

Lloyd Baird, Mentor

Lloyd Baird is Professor of Management at Boston University and Chair of the Organizational Behavior Department. He is also currently a principal at the Systems Research Center and Research Director of the Executive Development Roundtable, which focuses on the role of executives and leadership development. Dr. Baird works with corporations on issues such as the risks and potential of corporate-wide learning, knowledge, and leadership initiatives as well as with executives to help them drive both personal and organization transformation. He received his BS degree from Utah State University and his MBA and PhD from Michigan State University.

Leading People: The Basics

The Challenge of Contemporary Leadership

The definition
of leadership is to have inspired,
energized followers.
—Warren G. Bennis

eadership used to be viewed as innate. Epitomized by heroic, Lone Ranger types, it was seen as a mystical blend of courage, charisma, and even a flair for the dramatic. But beyond those traits, to paraphrase Louis Armstrong, if you had to ask what leadership was, you'd never know.

Fortunately, we've all grown wiser—or at least, we've had the lesson drummed into us by a business climate that is increasingly competitive and volatile. Yes, leadership still calls for courage and decisiveness in the face of conflicting demands. For example, the ability to make tradeoffs between people, resources, money, and deadlines—often causing short-term pain for the sake of long-term benefit—remains a vital element of effective leadership. But the changing structure of organizations, the growth of alliances and joint ventures between organizations, indeed, the changing nature of work itself—all call for more practical and diverse approaches to leadership.

Expand your leadership skills

There will always be a time and place for charismatic leaders, but few leaders today use formal authority and the power to command and control; rather, they *influence* and *motivate* people to achieve clearly defined goals. The power to influence and motivate requires skills such as:

- Communication skills to speak and write persuasively

- Interpersonal skills to listen and hear what people are really saying

- Conflict-resolution skills to handle the inevitable times of friction and tension

- Negotiation skills to bring differing groups together

- Motivational skills to convince people to strive for the same goal

Management versus Leadership Skills

MANAGEMENT SKILLS	LEADERSHIP SKILLS
Planning and budgeting	Setting a direction
Organizing and staffing	Aligning people to a vision
Controlling and problem solving	Motivating and inspiring

Leading or managing?

Are leadership skills the same skills effective managers use? Yes, to a degree. Managing and leading are complementary and often overlapping activities. The primary difference is that managing involves coping with complexity; leading, coping with *change.* At the same time, managing requires leadership skills, and leading requires management skills.

Management skills will always be essential, but in responding and adapting to the changing socioeconomic realities of today's markets, managers, even middle managers, are increasingly being called upon to be leaders as well.

Recognize the leadership challenge

No matter what the current economic, political, and social realities may be, the challenge for leaders today is to define their special goals or vision, to acquire as many management and leadership skills as possible, and, finally, to know when to use them to influence others to reach those goals.

What Makes an Effective Leader?

The cult of the heroic leader remains strong.

—Loren Gary, editor

E ffective leaders are not born with the gift of knowing how to lead. Rather, they gain experience, they absorb knowledge, they see and listen to the world around them—both inside the organization and beyond. Effective leaders are also capable of assuming the leadership qualities needed for specific situations. There are many kinds of effective leaders—among them the charismatic leader, the transformational leader, and the pragmatic leader—but these distinctive qualities can blend together in one person in different ways at different times.

Charismatic leaders seem to shine

A charismatic leader may seem to be born with a gift to inspire. Particularly during a crisis, people turn to this powerful voice for a grand vision and hope for solutions. Such a leader can clarify the situation for his people and instill the confidence they need. People feel safe handing off a problem to this type of leader.

What makes charismatic leaders such champions? They differ from the norm in greater self-confidence, energy, enthusiasm, and unconventional behavior. Charismatic leaders tend to:

- have a clear, fresh, new, and creative vision

- be completely devoted to their vision

- make great sacrifices to achieve their vision, taking personal risks—financial, professional, social

- create a sense of urgency among their followers

- gain the absolute trust of their followers (and also fear)

- use persuasion rather than forceful commands or democratic appeals for consensus to influence their followers

A charismatic leader is most successful during a crisis. For example, Franklin Delano Roosevelt was a charismatic leader who led the United States out of the Great Depression and readied the nation for World War II. On the other hand, Adolf Hitler was also a charismatic leader who gave his defeated nation a new vision of power and might. Thus, charismatic leaders can have great power and influence, but how they use it determines whether their inspiration works for good or not.

However, most organizations are not in a continual state of peril. A lofty vision for achieving a grand mission may not be attainable, and the value of inspiration may dissolve into a need for everyday, step-by-step progress. Thus, charismatic leaders are not always the best type of leader.

> *"[The charismatic leader is] supposed to have the 'gift of tongues,' with which he [can] inspire employees to work harder and gain the confidence of investors, analysts, and the ever skeptical press."*
> —Rakesh Khurana, professor

Transformational leaders focus on the people and the task

Unlike charismatic leaders, transformational leaders remold an organization not through the force of their own personality but by appealing to their people, gaining their trust and respect. Transformational leaders achieve results by paying close attention to their group or team as they

- articulate a clear and compelling vision

- clarify the importance of the vision's outcome

- provide a well-defined path to attain the vision

- use symbols to realize their vision

- act with confidence, optimism, and self-determination

- encourage their people to work as a team rather than as individuals to reach the organization's goals

- empower people to make good decisions for the benfit of the whole

What makes transformational leaders effective is their ability to make their vision a clear, identifiable goal that can guide their team's actions to meet that goal. They trust their people, provide the resources they need, and encourage them to move forward.

"It was Sacagawea, a Shoshone teenager, who led the Lewis and Clark expedition over its most perilous routes. But you also have to remember that Lewis must have been a great leader also, because he was willing to turn over the leadership and follow a young Indian who seemed to know what she was doing, but whom he had never met before."
—Douglas T. Hall, Director of the Executive Development Roundtable

Pragmatic leaders—from the ideal to the real

The most apparent characteristic of pragmatic leaders is their focus on the organization rather than on people. Pragmatic leaders face the realities of business environment; they listen to and understand the truth, whether good or bad, hopeful or daunting. They are effective because they

- have a vision that is recognizable as a variation of the status quo

- listen carefully to their people

- make realistic decisions for the good of the organization

- manage by the numbers

- put the right people in the right positions to get the job done

- delegate responsibilities to people they can trust

Pragmatic leaders may not be as flamboyant or exciting as other types of leaders, but they get the job done. Pragmatic leaders are most effective when an organization is going through rough times or when the business environment is too turbulent to see far ahead, when a short-term, familiar vision is necessary.

After all, Meriwether Lewis and William Clark were successful in attaining the goal of their Northwest journey. When they reached the Pacific Ocean in April 1805, Lewis wrote that he was "much pleased at having arrived at this long wished for spot."

Effective leaders are future-focused

In general, leaders who are effective now and in the future have learned how to be:

- future-focused. They create a vision, articulate it to their group, and stick with it. They understand how their unit or organization fits into the larger picture, and they organize short-term tasks according to long-term priorities.

- comfortable with ambiguity. They are willing to take calculated risks, can handle a certain level of disruption and conflict, and are willing to change their minds when new information comes to light.

- persistent. They can maintain a positive, focused determination in pursuing a goal or vision, despite the obstacles.

- excellent communicators. They know how to write clearly, listen closely, run meetings, make presentations, negotiate, and speak in public.

- politically astute. They have acquired a solid sense of their organization's power structure, listen carefully to the concerns of its most powerful groups, and know where to turn for the support and resources they need.

- level-headed. They know how to stay calm in the midst of turmoil and confusion.

- self-aware. They know themselves enough to realize how their own patterns of behavior affect others.

- caring. They have a demonstrated ability to empathize with other people's needs, concerns, and professional goals.

- humorous. When the situation warrants it, they know how to inject a little mirth to relieve tension within a group.

Tip: Be the change you want to bring about—model the behaviors you're trying to encourage.

Self-Evaluation: Characteristics of Effective Leadership

The questions below relate to characteristics of effective leaders. Use the questions to evaluate whether you possess these characteristics. Use the results to see where you might focus to strengthen your leadership skills.

Characteristics of Effective Leaders	Yes	No
Future-focused		
1. Do you have a clear vision?	✓	
2. Have you made your vision clear to your group?	✓	
Persistent; tenacious		
3. When pursuing a goal, do you maintain a positive, focused attitude, despite obstacles?	✓	
Comfortable with ambiguity		
4. Are you willing to take calculated risks?	✓	
5. Are you comfortable with a certain level of disruption and conflict?	✓	
Excellent communicators		
6. Do you listen closely (rather than have a response ready before the other person finishes)?		✓
7. Are you comfortable running meetings?	✓	
8. Are you comfortable making presentations and speaking in public?	✓	
9. Do you have the skills needed to negotiate in a variety of settings?		✓
Politically astute		
10. Could you diagram for yourself your organization's actual power structure?	✓	
11. Can you articulate the concerns of your organization's most powerful groups?	✓	

Characteristics of Effective Leaders	Yes	No
12. Can you identify those individuals within your organization who will support you when needed?	✓	
13. Do you know where to turn for the resources you need?	✓	
Self-aware		
14. Are you aware of or can you describe how your own patterns of behavior affect others?		✓
Level-headed		
15. In situations that are full of turmoil and confusion, do you stay calm and level-headed?		✓
Caring		
16. Do you empathize with other people's needs, concerns, and professional goals?		✓
17. Would staff members confirm that you show such empathy?		✓
Able to use humor		
18. Do you know how to use humor to relieve tense or uncomfortable situations?	✓	
*If you answered **"yes"** to most of these questions, you have the characteristics of an effective leader.* *If you answered **"no"** to some or many of these questions, you may want to consider how you can further develop these effective leadership characteristics.*		

How to Acquire Leadership Skills

Becoming a leader does not occur by osmosis. If you want to be a leader, you need to work at it. You probably have some of the skills mastered already. You may have excellent communication skills, or you already have a pretty good idea of what your vision is. You may even have that gift to inspire others. But if you lack some skills, knowledge, or experience, go out and get them!

Be aggressive about becoming a leader

How? Here are some suggestions:

Enroll in formal leadership programs. There are plenty of management training programs; aim for the ones designed specifically for leaders. Offered by consulting companies or universities, these programs may include focused weekend workshops or yearlong programs that cover the whole range of leadership skills. The training techniques may vary from case discussions and role playing to games that simulate analytical or decision-making situations.

Learn from experience. Even here, however, don't learn passively. Think strategically about how you will gain the experience you need. Here are some ways to gain real leadership experience:

- Ask to be assigned to challenging projects that will provide new and unusual problems to solve, such as joining a cross-functional team or a team working on a merger or acquisition.

- Stay alert. Try to observe situations from different perspectives. Watch how different people approach and solve similar problems.

- Don't be afraid to fail. You probably learn more from failing once or twice than from succeeding all the time. The important thing is to take responsibility for your failure and recognize how you could do better the next time.

- Get involved in a variety of assignments; don't just do the same old tasks over and over again.

- Ask for feedback. Find out from others how you are doing. Be open to helpful criticism.

- Elect to join job rotation programs. These programs can help you develop your managerial, technical, business, and communication skills in diverse roles.

Find a true mentor. Mentoring may seem like an excellent source for gaining knowledge about leadership, but the results have been mixed. The mentor should have the experience you want to gain, a genuine willingness to help you along, and a positive relationship with you.

Learn to adapt to different leadership styles

The key to getting the most from all these leadership learning activities is to coordinate them. Know what knowledge, skills, and experiences you need, and plan how to acquire them in an integrated fashion.

What Would YOU Do?

The Prince and the Pauper

A S HIS TAILOR PINNED THE cuff of his new pants, Joseph speculated that Tariq must have some special "in." You'd never know that the two of them had been promoted at the same time. What a difference! Tariq had lunches sent in while he ran meetings in the executive conference room. He chatted up division heads in their offices and strolled the halls with the top people from other departments. Joseph worked like a horse, crunching budgets, making Gantt charts, running team meetings, and hiring new staff. But none of his hard work was bringing him any recognition. The meeting this morning was humiliating. Every time Tariq made a point, everyone nodded in agreement. When Joseph talked, they asked him a lot of questions, as if they didn't quite trust him. Joseph looked in the mirror and wondered if wearing suits like Tariq's would be enough . . . or was there something else he ought to be doing?

Leadership styles are behavioral adaptations to particular situations. Effective leaders learn, practice, and master each of the six leadership styles. Even though these leadership styles are presented as distinct behaviors, they often overlap as needed.

Leadership Styles

STYLE	CHARACTERISTICS	WHEN USEFUL	WEAKNESSES
Coercive	Leader gives orders and expects to be obeyed.	Turnaround situations Natural or manmade disasters Dealing with difficult or problem employees	Inhibits organization's flexibility Weakens employee motivation
Authoritative	Leader establishes overall goal and pushes people to follow.	Business is adrift and needs direction. Business is in a downturn.	Leader's goal may not be the best one. Experts may disagree with the leader.
Affiliative	Leader assumes a "people come first" attitude.	Need to build team cohesion Need to raise low morale	May allow poor employee performance to continue unchecked Employees may not have a sense of direction.
Democratic	Leader gives employees role in decision making.	Need to build organizational flexibility and responsibility	May result in indecision and a sense of confusion
Pacesetting	Leader sets high performance standards.	Highly motivated employees can work on their own.	May feel overwhelming for employees who cannot attain the high standards Some employees may feel resentful.
Coaching	Leader focuses on personal development.	Employees want to change and improve professionally.	Not successful when employees are resistant to change.

You may find some styles more comfortable than others, but the more you can develop a range of styles, the more effectively you will perform as a leader.

Tip: Adapt your leadership style to the needs of your people. Give latitude to those who can handle delegation; provide coaching to those whose skills and confidence need a boost; give explicit directions to those who need close supervision.

What You COULD Do.

Remember Joseph's dilemma?

Here's what the mentor suggests:

Is there something else Joseph should be doing? Yes. He needs to figure out what he really wants. There is a difference between being a manager and being a leader. Managers execute and get things done. Leaders determine what needs to be done. Both are valuable, and anyone can do either or both. But Joseph needs to decide which one he will be.

Joseph should not be fooled by appearances. Tariq may be playing the political game, not the leadership game. In the short term, he may get away with it. In the long term, it will catch him if he is not producing results. Let's assume Tariq is playing the leadership game. He is spending his time working with others to set direction, focusing people and resources on that direction, and worrying about how to build the coalition and energy to get the vision implemented. If that is the case, it is no wonder people are listening to him and involving him in important meetings.

Joseph is spending his time crunching the numbers, preparing the reports, and hiring new staff, all to accomplish the objectives others have set. He is performing technical and managerial work. Both are very valuable, and he may be best suited and happiest performing that type of work. But he should not make the mistake of assuming that working hard and producing results with a managerial focus will qualify him to be a leader. Leaders have a different set of skills. These skills can be developed, but they take constant focus and work.

How to
Craft a Vision

A vision is a mind-picture of your hoped-for end result: what it will look like, how it will function, what it will produce, and how things will be changed by it. A simple, clear, and enduring vision of a better future is a leader's most important motivational tool; you'll refer to it time and again, explaining its benefits and relevance to various audiences as you work to keep them on board. The result of broad-based strategic thinking about the company's most key constituencies and a willingness to take calculated risks, a vision doesn't need to be brilliant or innovative. In fact, some of the best can seem mundane.

Where does your vision fit into the organizational scheme?

In the professional world, the word *vision* has been confused with other important concepts, such as *mission statement, strategic objective,* or *slogans.* But a vision, though related to these other concepts, overarches them and gives them meaning.

What comprises a clearly stated, empowering vision?

A vision provides a clear picture of a better future. It offers trust, faith, and hope for everyone in the organization. It becomes a guide for an organization to move from past beliefs, activities, and goals to a future path more suited to the changing needs of the organization and the demands of the economic environment.

A vision should be

- simple and idealistic. It should appeal to core values of the organization.
- challenging but realistic. It's fine for the vision to have lofty language—you want it to be large enough to touch people's core needs for achievement, recognition, and a sense of belonging. But the lofty language has to be easily translated into a realistic competitive strategy. The goals can be aggressive, but they must also be achievable.
- focused. It should serve as a guide in decision making
- beneficial for the organization's stakeholders—customers, stockholders, and employees. It should clearly define the benefits to these various constituencies.
- easy to explain and understand. Even if *implementing* the vision is a complicated process, explaining it should be simple. People won't support what they can't understand.

"When the road ahead is unclear, vision can take you only so far."
   —Loren Gary, editor

Develop your vision

You may have a general notion of where you would like your organization to go, but to craft a vision, take the following steps to ensure as much buy-in from stakeholders as possible.

What Would YOU Do?

Great Expectations

WHEN JESSICA TOOK OVER THE DEPARTMENT, she knew that her job was to take it right into the twenty-first century. So she was frustrated with Mary, her mentor and boss, for not giving her the support she needed. They had just finished discussing the new direction for the department for the fourth time. Jessica was starting to feel that Mary was holding out on her. "Where do you see the department going?" she would ask, and Mary would turn the question right back around. "Where do *you* see your department going?" she'd reply. Sometimes she'd make a vague suggestion or offer an encouraging remark, but that wasn't what Jessica was looking for. Why wouldn't Mary tell her what she was supposed to be doing? After all, Mary was the boss! She was supposed to be the one with the grand vision, wasn't she?

Consider first the shared values and ideals of the organization. You won't get very far if you don't adhere to the basic beliefs of the group. Retain whatever is still useful and valuable from the former vision and mission. You don't always have to throw out the entire past to move forward.

A STRATEGIC OBJECTIVE IS RELATED TO A MISSION STATEMENT IS RELATED TO A VISION: THE BIG DIG IN BOSTON, MASSACHUSETTS

A *vision* not only captures *what* the organization does but it expresses *why* the organization exists. A *vision* breathes life into a mission statement. It communicates an image of what can be achieved and why it is a good thing to achieve.

The Central Artery Tunnel Project (Big Dig) is the largest, most complex, and technologically challenging highway project ever attempted in American history. The project will dramatically reduce traffic congestion and improve mobility in one of America's oldest and most congested cities, improve the environment, and lay the groundwork for continued economic growth for millions of New Englanders in the coming new century.

A *mission statement* describes the purpose of the organization by articulating what it does.

To resolve the major traffic problems and endangered quality of life in Boston and New England, we will replace the elevated highway with an underground highway and extend I-90 through a tunnel to Logan Airport.

A *strategic objective* is a near-term tangible outcome, not an enduring reason for being.

The I-90 connector from the MassPike extension to the Ted Williams Tunnel will be completed by January 20, 2003.

A *slogan* is a quick summary.

The Big Dig: Worth the Wait.

"A Buddhist monk once said, 'When you wash dishes, wash dishes.' At first the monk's zen-like thought seemed obvious to me, of no particular value, but upon reflection it began to make more sense. Eventually, I translated it into a phrase that had great significance: 'When in charge, be in charge.' And being in charge means that you must create the future."

—Gordon Sullivan, Chief of Staff, U.S. Army (retired)

Discuss your ideas with various stakeholders. Talk to your superiors and subordinates, and use lateral networking to get valuable information, input, and early support across various functions and departments. Find out what they want and need, and, most importantly, how they react to your vision.

Make sure that all perspectives are represented. Failure to listen to a powerful group or voice can result in problems later on. For example, certain stakeholders may be unwilling to support you at a critical juncture. If you don't incorporate the opinion of an important group, your vision may not address all relevant organizational needs.

Use the results of your research wisely. Incorporate what you learned to define a vision that is both realistic and focused. An effective vision is achievable. Even if it is ambitious, you, your team, and your stakeholders need to be imagining the same set of outcomes.

Ask your team to provide reality checks to help clarify the vision. Listen to those closest to you. Remain flexible. You may have to keep reassessing and revising your vision until it's right.

Clearly define the vision's benefits to all involved. Determine the benefits not only to your unit, but to the broader organization—employees, stockholders, and customers alike. If these stakeholders know "what's in it for me," they'll be more likely to embrace the vision and offer assistance when asked.

Think in terms of satisfying deep human needs. People want to achieve; they want to feel that they belong; they want to have self-esteem and a feeling of control over their lives. If your vision helps to satisfy these needs, you will have plenty of support.

What You COULD Do.

Remember Jessica's dilemma?

Here's what the mentor suggests:

There is a difference between boss-ship and leadership. The boss is the one who holds the organization accountable for accomplishing the organization's objectives. The leader, on the other hand, is the one who influences others to accomplish a common goal. Often in organizations today, the boss will not be able to be clear about goals; after all, the environment is changing too fast.

Jessica probably knows more about her job than her boss does. She should set the vision herself, check it out with her boss, and get on with it. Of course she will make mistakes, but she will learn as she goes and make necessary adjustments. The biggest mistake Jessica can make is waiting for the boss to tell her what her objectives should be. She needs to figure out where her department is going, get buy-in from her boss, and keep her informed of the progress she is making; by doing this, Jessica becomes the leader.

Jessica might ask herself: "If I were to go to one of my direct reports, do you think he would say, 'We are very clear where we are going and what we are supposed to accomplish'? Or would his response be, 'Why won't Jessica just tell us what we are supposed to be doing'?" Would your direct reports be clear about what you want from them? Are you a leader or a follower?

Worksheet for Crafting and Maintaining Your Vision

Complete this worksheet to create a "picture" of your hoped-for vision: what it will look like, how it will function, what it will produce. Use the results to maintain a record of your vision and help sell it to others.

1. Gather Information for the Vision

Write a general description of the hoped-for end result.
I want to expand my successful product into a product line and a recognized brand name.

What information is necessary to define the vision in detail?
I need to survey current customers to see what additional features or variations they would be interested in purchasing.

Who across the organization can provide information, input, and early support? What do you need to ask them?
My department head has to agree to this expansion. I need information and cooperation from marketing and sales.

Input and ideas:
I will meet with the head of the new products department. I'll also ask colleagues from other companies what they think of my ideas.

Who might oppose this effort? What questions do you need to ask them?
Other product managers who have unsuccessful products. I will ask them to share ideas and perhaps include some version of their products.

The finance VP might not approve the extra resources needed. I'll ask him what kind of pro forma she needs to approve the plan.

Feedback:
I need feedback from customers and colleagues. Sales team has a good sense of the market, so I'll ask them for feedback.

2. Craft the Vision

Articulate the vision.
My product line will become a familiar brand for consumers who expect the best and get it from us. My products will satisfy the customers and increase in sales and profitability each fiscal year.

continued

2. Craft the Vision, *continued*

What is your overall strategy to reach the vision?
Once I have done my homework and collected all the data possible, I will present the business plan to the executive committee.

If they agree to the full expansion, I'll start immediately with designing the line extensions.

3. Checklist: Is Your Vision Realistic?	Yes	No
1. Have team members contributed to the vision and given "buy-in"?	✓	
2. Is the vision realistic and achievable?	✓	
3. Does the end-result of the vision serve the interests of the company's most important stakeholders?	✓	
4. Does the vision include a clear definition of the benefits to all the constituencies that might be affected?	✓	
5. Is the language used in the vision documentation easy to explain and understand?	✓	
6. Does the description of the vision include and articulate a wide range of perspectives (of all affected stakeholders)?	✓	

If you answer "no" to any question, revisit the vision and adjust it to include that aspect.

How to
Motivate the People
You Need

To ensure that your vision is embraced and fulfilled, you have to pay attention to the people around you—those who will help and those who may hinder your progress. Take care to handle both the political and the personal sides of leading and implementing your vision.

Watch the political scene closely

What do you need to be aware of within your organization? Any leader who wants to make major changes pays attention to her surroundings, understands the changing politics of her world, and marks the realignments that may take place.

Know who could hinder you or help you. Take the time necessary to identify those who might resist you in some way—for example, by blocking your access to needed resources. Plan how you will deal with such problems. Work to win over those key people who aren't enthusiastically behind you or who for some reason may feel threatened by you and your vision.

Build a broad coalition within the organization and among the stakeholders. An effective leader has to be a persuasive communicator. Building coalitions is when this skill becomes particularly useful. You will need cooperation from people at all levels of your organization and beyond (for example, suppliers, contractors, clients, etc.).

Choose carefully whom you assign to important roles. People in key positions need to be competent in their roles and loyal to your vision.

Do something dramatic or bold to shake things up. If the changes you are making are significant, then make sure everyone is involved and understands what's happening. If you are realigning the company's organizational structure, for example, do it quickly and fairly.

Or, if necessary, take tiny steps at first. You may not be able to make dramatic changes simultaneously. There may be technical or political barriers. But even if you can make only small changes that show success, you'll be on your way. Any movement toward your vision should be noted as positive.

Tip: Protect those who voice dissent within the group—they are often sources of new and better ideas for getting the job done.

Care for your people

The people within your own group—whether that group is a company, department, or team—are critical for achieving your vision. Motivating them, caring for them, and leading them is your primary duty.

What Would YOU Do?

War and Peace

HANNAH WAS A PEACEFUL PERSON, and she was ready to call a truce to end the war being waged in her department. Every time she asked her people to agree on a direction, it seemed they understood this as a signal to attack. One group would come up with a plan, and the other would knock it down. Someone else would hurl out another idea, and then everyone would ride roughshod over that. Reaching agreement over what to do was only a preliminary skirmish. Then a "take-no-prisoners" battle would ensue over the means of getting there. By the time her troops finally reached an agreement, Hannah was exhausted. They, on the other hand, seemed energized and ready to move on to the next issue. How could she put a stop to this combat? She considered setting a time limit on the discussions. Or taking sides. Or making the decisions herself. After all, there couldn't be any value to such excruciating conflicts, could there?

Make sure they are with you. Once you are certain your people understand the vision, the mission, and the steps to be taken en route, create a sense of urgency about your shared endeavors. Keep your people excited about what they're doing.

Be prepared for resistance to change. Most people dislike change, even when they know the change is for the better. Rather than ignore that fear of change, recognize and deal with it openly.

Acknowledge and celebrate successes. And continue to celebrate successes, right up to the end. Celebrations can be large and small. A cheer for all, a lunch or picnic, t-shirts or caps—anything to keep spirits up.

Keep people informed. People don't like feeling excluded from the news of progress or of problems. By keeping your people updated, they will be ready to help solve problems as they arise.

Remain committed to the vision. Your commitment will be a model for everyone in the group. If they see you working hard to attain the goals, they will join you.

Empower your people to develop their own leadership skills. The benefits of supporting and trusting others can be enormous. You will gain loyalty as well as experienced and productive employees.

Create a trusting environment

A work environment based on trust allows the individuals of a group to become a cohesive team, working toward the vision for the benefit of all. To achieve this kind of environment,

- Treat everyone, at every level of the hierarchy, with respect and consideration.

- Give everyone's ideas serious consideration.

- Be fair, kind, and courteous at all times.

- Never put other people down.

- Be honest. Admit it when you make a mistake or when you don't have the answer.

- Protect your group. Define a boundary around your group and shelter them from interference. Go to bat for your team to get the resources you need. Show courage in sticking up for your people.

- Do not tolerate scapegoating or misapplied blame.

- Use every reasonable opportunity to foster others' professional growth.

The value of creating this atmosphere is worth the extra effort it may entail because it can

- reinforce trust among team members

- bring people together so they can focus on issues

- help you regulate the friction that is often necessary to do the job

- uphold principles of mutual respect and consideration

- focus on behavior, not personality

- give workers a sense of purpose

- create opportunities for others' professional growth

- foster a positive attitude

- protect a team's members

The result will be that your people will trust and believe you. Credibility is imperative if you are to lead people and achieve your vision.

"You can't believe how many times I'd be sitting home replaying a game I had just played. I'd watch myself come off a pick, and I'd see Danny Ainge, wide open in the corner, and I'd say to myself, "Geez, how did I miss him?" Then I'd go in the next day and say to Danny, "Hey, you were wide open on that play last night in the third quarter. My fault. Call for me next time, and I'll get you the ball."
—Larry Bird, basketball player and coach

Adapt your leadership style to the needs of your people

The members of your group will have different capabilities, needs, and growth potential. Stay flexible in dealing with them; try to respond to them in ways that address their particular needs and interests.

- Be direct with people who are just learning a new skill. They need very specific instructions and ongoing feedback.

- Support people who are learning skills but are still gaining experience. They need direction, but also the freedom to make some mistakes and encouragement to keep going.

- Encourage people who may be highly competent, but who may lack self-confidence. Use positive reinforcement to help them recognize their developing abilities.

- Delegate to highly motivated and experienced people. Don't just delegate work that you find unpleasant. Determine whose expertise or personal experience is suited to a "stretch" assignment, then give that person the freedom and support she needs to succeed.

LEADING AND MOTIVATING TOOLS

Establishing Credibility

Use this checklist to evaluate how well you are able to establish credibility and to create a prodcutive working environment.

Checklist for Establishing Credibility	Yes	No
1. Do you have, and can you demonstrate competence in a particular area?	✓	
2. Do you demonstrate your willingness to work hard on a day-to-day basis?	✓	
3. Do you use whatever power and influence you have to benefit others?	✓	
4. Do you consciously treat everyone with whom you come in contact consistently and fairly?		✓
5. Do you focus on practicing active listening on a day-to-day basis?		✓
6. Do you keep track of and deliver on all promises you make?		✓
7. Do you consistently meet deadlines?		✓
8. Do you remain calm under pressure?		✓

Checklist for Establishing Credibility	Yes	No
9. Do you prepare thoroughly for meetings and presentations?		✓
10. Do you answer all phone calls and respond to all e-mails promptly?	✓	
11. Do you keep accurate and detailed records of projects and activities?	✓	
12. Would colleagues at any level say they have never heard you put another person down?	✓	
13. Do you show that you will not tolerate "scapegoating," or misapplied blame?	✓	
14. Do you listen fairly, kindly and with courtesy to the opinions of others?		✓
15. Do you respect other people's ideas and give each one the same amount of consideration, regardless of level?		✓
16. Do you go to bat for your team to get the resources you need?	✓	
17. Do you shelter your team from interference and show courage in sticking up for your people?	✓	
18. Do you protect voices of dissent, and leaders who are working without authority?	✓	
19. Do you admit it when you make a mistake or when you don't have the answer?	✓	
20. Do you use every reasonable opportunity to foster other's professional growth?	✓	

*If you answer "**yes**" to most of these questions, you are probably doing a good job of establishing your credibility and building a productive work environment.*

*If you answer "**no**" to any questions, you may want to focus on how to improve your performance in that area. Identify how to change your behavior and practice it until it becomes second nature.*

What You COULD Do.

Remember Hannah's dilemma?

Here's what the mentor suggests:

Individuals have to decide the style of leadership they prefer. Then they have to decide how to vary their style based on the situation they face. Sometimes you try to change the situation; sometimes you try to change your style. Either can be effective. Hannah has decisions to make. Does she want the group to learn how to solve their own conflicts? Does she want to be more authoritarian and drive the decisions herself? Is the situation such that she needs to make decisions quickly? How will she get buy-in on the decisions that are made?

What Hannah cannot do is let the situation continue as it is. If she wants her group to learn how to work together better, she will have to get in there and help them understand how to resolve conflicts and solve problems. She may have to reorganize the groups. Or she could change the reward systems so they succeed most when everyone succeeds. If she needs decisions made quickly, she may need to become more aggressive about managing input and make the decisions herself. Leadership is about choices. Hannah has to choose what style fits her best and what style best fits the situation.

Keeping Staff and Allies Motivated

Complete this worksheet regularly to track how motivated staff and allies are and to consider how well you are using available strategies to keep them motivated.

Date: January 20

Staff morale is down *(Up? Down? Flat? Mixed?)* **because** the post-holiday slump has hurt our numbers.

Successes or major milestones we have achieved so far:

1. We launched the improved, top-of-the line product. Reception has been slow but positive.

2. We've regrouped the staff so that people with experience in the area are represented on each team.

3. The third tier, lower cost product is in the testing stage, two weeks ahead of schedule.

Individuals who have been instrumental in success to date and what motivates them:

Sian has been creative and enthusiastic. She just believes in the whole project. Martin works hard and produces, but he's too concerned about his status within the group. Marta has been terrific as a source of outside support. She seems to enjoy helping, but she's also networking.

Reward ideas for group:

We need a morale booster. The plan is to provide breakfast every Friday during February. They might even have more energy if they start the day eating instead of dashing about.

Aspects of the "big picture" to emphasize at this point in the effort:

Need to plan a group meeting to celebrate how quickly we're moving along in product development. That should encourage those folks in marketing and sales who haven't seen the payback yet.

continued

Checklist: How Well Are You Maintaining Motivation?	Yes	No
1. Have you offered feedback and recognition to individuals who have been instrumental in successes to date?	✓	
2. Have you reported to the team and allies about successes achieved so far and how they relate to the big picture?		✓
3. Have you celebrated successes and the accomplishment of major milestones?		✓
4. Have you spoken recently about the team's ability to overcome problems?	✓	
5. Have you spoken to team members about the importance of their work and how it relates to the company's or unit's larger goals?	✓	
6. Have you remembered to offer special rewards, such as food at team meetings or achievement awards?	✓	
If you answer "no" to any question, consider adjusting your leadership strategies.		

How to Care
for Yourself

Leadership is principally concerned with key tasks and perspectives—but it also has its personal side. Neglect yourself and your own needs, and you'll soon be overwhelmed by the pressures that build on those in leadership positions.

How can you care for yourself?

There are several things—small and large—you can do to avoid the darker side of leadership—the stress that often accompanies the role. The fact that you are succeeding in your career and that your leadership and vision are bringing benefits to the organization should ease your mind. Nevertheless, be wise and try these stress-relieving tactics

- Talk regularly with a confidant—for example, a spouse or trusted friend—about your chief concerns at work.

- If you don't have a mentor, get one. You should be mentored by at least one relatively senior and influential guiding light who is invested in your development and success, and whose advice you can trust without hesitation.

- Take advantage of professional development seminars that help you refine your leadership skills.

- Find a sanctuary, a place you can go to at regular intervals that affords you "a view from the balcony": the chance to reflect on overarching patterns and issues in your work life.

- Don't take things personally if someone criticizes you. As the leader, you're often the lightning rod for other issues.

- Practice relaxation techniques such as deep breathing, taking a short walk, or stretching your body.

- Don't forget to exercise regularly—it relieves stress, helps you sleep better, and gives you more energy.

Tip: Acknowledge the stress you feel.

The burdens of leadership can be daunting.

And remember: Delegation is not a sign of weakness. It makes you a better leader, develops the potential of your staff, and helps you avoid burnout. So, go ahead, shed some tasks. Delegate to subordinates whatever responsibilities you can, but don't pass off just the tedious tasks. Once you've delegated a task, make sure not to let it get pushed back up to you.

Tip: Keep telling yourself that what you

are doing is valuable.

Tips and Tools

Tools for Leading People

Self-Evaluation: Characteristics of Effective Leadership

The questions below relate to characteristics of effective leaders. Use the questions to evaluate whether you possess these characteristics. Use the results to see where you might focus to strengthen your leadership skills.

Characteristics of Effective Leaders	Yes	No
Future-focused		
1. Do you have a clear vision?		
2. Have you made your vision clear to your group?		
Persistent; tenacious		
3. When pursuing a goal, do you maintain a positive, focused attitude, despite obstacles?		
Comfortable with ambiguity		
4. Are you willing to take calculated risks?		
5. Are you comfortable with a certain level of disruption and conflict?		
Excellent communicators		
6. Do you listen closely (rather than have a response ready before the other person finishes)?		
7. Are you comfortable running meetings?		
8. Are you comfortable making presentations and speaking in public?		
9. Do you have the skills needed to negotiate in a variety of settings?		
Politically astute		
10. Could you diagram for yourself your organization's actual power structure?		
11. Can you articulate the concerns of your organization's most powerful groups?		
12. Can you identify those individuals within your organization who will support you when needed?		
13. Do you know where to turn for the resources you need?		

Characteristics of Effective Leaders	Yes	No
Self-aware		
14. Are you aware of or can you describe how your own patterns of behavior affect others?		
Level-headed		
15. In situations that are full of turmoil and confusion, do you stay calm and level-headed?		
Caring		
16. Do you empathize with other people's needs, concerns, and professional goals?		
17. Would staff members confirm that you show such empathy?		
Able to use humor		
18. Do you know how to use humor to relieve tense or uncomfortable situations?		

If you answered "yes" to most of these questions, you have the characteristics of an effective leader.

If you answered "no" to some or many of these questions, you may want to consider how you can further develop these effective leadership characteristics.

Worksheet for Crafting and Maintaining Your Vision

Complete this worksheet to create a "picture" of your hoped-for vision: what it will look like, how it will function, what it will produce. Use the results to maintain a record of your vision and help sell it to others.

1. Gather Information for the Vision

Write a general description of the hoped-for end result.

What information is necessary to define the vision in detail?

Who across the organization can provide information, input, and early support? What do you need to ask them?

Input and ideas:

Who might oppose this effort? What questions do you need to ask them?

Feedback:

2. Craft the Vision

Articulate the vision.

What is your overall strategy to reach the vision?

3. Checklist: Is Your Vision Realistic?	Yes	No
1. Have team members contributed to the vision and given "buy-in"?		
2. Is the vision realistic and achievable?		
3. Does the end-result of the vision serve the interests of the company's most important stakeholders?		
4. Does the vision include a clear definition of the benefits to all the constituencies that might be affected?		
5. Is the language used in the vision documentation easy to explain and understand?		
6. Does the description of the vision include and articulate a wide range of perspectives (of all affected stakeholders)?		
*If you answer **"no"** to any question, revisit the vision and adjust it to include that aspect.*		

Establishing Credibility

*Use this checklist to evaluate how well you are able to establish
credibility and to create a prodcutive working environment.*

Checklist for Establishing Credibility	Yes	No
1. Do you have, and can you demonstrate competence in a particular area?		
2. Do you demonstrate your willingness to work hard on a day-to-day basis?		
3. Do you use whatever power and influence you have to benefit others?		
4. Do you consciously treat everyone with whom you come in contact consistently and fairly?		
5. Do you focus on practicing active listening on a day-to-day basis?		
6. Do you keep track of and deliver on all promises you make?		
7. Do you consistently meet deadlines?		
8. Do you remain calm under pressure?		
9. Do you prepare thoroughly for meetings and presentations?		
10. Do you answer all phone calls and respond to all e-mails promptly?		
11. Do you keep accurate and detailed records of projects and activities?		
12. Would colleagues at any level say they have never heard you put another person down?		
13. Do you show that you will not tolerate "scapegoating," or misapplied blame?		
14. Do you listen fairly, kindly and with courtesy to the opinions of others?		
15. Do you respect other people's ideas and give each one the same amount of consideration, regardless of level?		

Checklist for Establishing Credibility	Yes	No
16. Do you go to bat for your team to get the resources you need?		
17. Do you shelter your team from interference and show courage in sticking up for your people?		
18. Do you protect voices of dissent, and leaders who are working without authority?		
19. Do you admit it when you make a mistake or when you don't have the answer?		
20. Do you use every reasonable opportunity to foster other's professional growth?		

*If you answer **"yes"** to most of these questions, you are probably doing a good job of establishing your credibility and building a productive work environment.*

*If you answer **"no"** to any questions, you may want to focus on how to improve your performance in that area. Identify how to change your behavior and practice it until it becomes second nature.*

Keeping Staff and Allies Motivated

Complete this worksheet regularly to track how motivated staff and allies are and to consider how well you are using available strategies to keep them motivated.

Date:

Staff morale is *(Up? Down? Flat? Mixed?)* **because**

Successes or major milestones we have achieved so far:

Individuals who have been instrumental in success to date and what motivates them:

Reward ideas for group:

Aspects of the "big picture" to emphasize at this point in the effort:

Checklist: How Well Are You Maintaining Motivation?	Yes	No
1. Have you offered feedback and recognition to individuals who have been instrumental in successes to date?		
2. Have you reported to the team and allies about successes achieved so far and how they relate to the big picture?		
3. Have you celebrated successes and the accomplishment of major milestones?		
4. Have you spoken recently about the team's ability to overcome problems?		
5. Have you spoken to team members about the importance of their work and how it relates to the company's or unit's larger goals?		
6. Have you remembered to offer special rewards, such as food at team meetings or achievement awards?		

*If you answer **"no"** to any question, consider adjusting your leadership strategies.*

Test Yourself

Test Yourself offers ten multiple-choice questions to help you identify your baseline knowledge of leading and motivating.

Answers to the questions are given at the end of the test.

1. As a leader, you should rely on others for help.

    a. True.

    b. False.

2. A leader's primary job is to

    a. Create a clear and enduring set of strategic objectives.

    b. Influence others.

    c. Meet the challenges of the future.

3. A charismatic leader is most successful during times when

    a. There is a downturn in the economy.

    b. The company is negotiating a merger.

    c. A labor strike threatens production.

4. To learn how to become a leader, you can

    a. Ask to take on challenging projects.

    b. Prepare by being the best manager you can.

    c. Find a mentor in a different field.

5. What is NOT a characteristic of an effective leader?

    a. Excellent communication skills.

    b. A sense of humor.

    c. Dislike of ambiguity.

6. You are focusing on developing your leadership skills. Is being politically astute about your organization's power structure and using what you know a characteristic of being an effective leader?

    a. Yes.

    b. No.

    c. Sometimes, but you don't want to rely on outsiders for support.

7. A democratic leadership style is characterized by

    a. Coaching talented direct reports.

    b. Achieving consensus in a group.

    c. Maintaining a "people first" approach to leading.

8. An effective leader's vision needs to be

   a. Daring and exciting.

   b. A goal that can never quite be reached.

   c. Simple and enduring.

9. To motivate people, a leader should

   a. Celebrate successes.

   b. Never allow any questioning of the vision.

   c. Be willing to adjust the vision as needed.

10. An effective leader

   a. Will never show emotions.

   b. Does not admit mistakes.

   c. Finds a sanctuary to let go and relax.

Answers to test questions

1, a. Yes, of course, you should rely on others. You can't do it all yourself. The people within your own group—whether that group is a company, department, or team—are critical for achieving your vision.

2, b. Leaders need to persuade, influence, and motivate others. A leader also creates a vision for change—strategic objectives follow the vision.

3, c. Charismatic leaders function best during a time of crisis, not during ongoing situations.

4, a. Find challenging projects to learn new ways of seeing problems and solutions. Don't just stay at the managerial level, and don't connect with an inappropriate mentor.

5, c. Leaders have to be comfortable with the unknown; ambiguity is an inherent element of the future, and leaders have to be future-focused.

6, a. Do be politically astute. Effective leaders know their organization's power structure. They listen carefully to concerns of centers of power, and they know where to go for resources and support they need.

7, b. A democratic leadership is characterized by a leader working to achieve consensus in a group, often a difficult task.

8, c. An effective leader will have a vision that others can understand and accept as bringing about a better future.

9, a. Celebrate successes, large and small, at the start, the middle and the end of the road.

10, c. Leaders need to take care of themselves. Often they work too hard and take on too much stress. Finding a quiet place to relax and unwind is important for a leader's mental health.

To Learn More

Notes and Articles

Loren Gary. "Power: How Its Meaning in Corporate Life Is Changing." *Harvard Management Update*, October 1996.

This article offers a review of current literature on power and the way power is used by both individuals and organizations. The author shows the psychological transition in equating power as "not the capacity to destroy, but rather, the ability to influence others." He discusses the ways in which power is applied in various management situations and how you can use power to transform your relationships with others in an organization.

Daniel Goleman. "Leadership That Gets Results." *Harvard Business Review* OnPoint Enhanced Edition. Boston: Harvard Business School Publishing, 2000.

Drawing on research on more than 3,000 executives, Goleman explores which precise leadership behaviors yield positive results. He outlines six distinct leadership styles, each one arising from different components of emotional intelligence. For example, coercive leaders demand immediate compliance. Authoritative leaders mobilize people toward a vision. Affiliative leaders create emotional bonds and harmony. Democratic leaders build consensus through participation. Pacesetting leaders expect excellence and self-direction. And coaching leaders develop people for the future. The research indicates that leaders who get the best results don't rely on just one leadership style; they use most of the styles in any given week. Goleman maintains that with practice leaders can switch among leadership styles to produce powerful results, thus turning the art of leadership into a skill that can be learned.

Daniel Goleman, Richard Boyatzis, and Annie Mckee. "Primal Leadership: The Hidden Driver of Great Performance." *Harvard Business Review* OnPoint Enhanced Edition. Boston: Harvard Business School Publishing, 2001.

You've heard about the importance of emotional intelligence in the workplace—that there's an incontrovertible link between executives' emotional maturity, exemplified by such capabilities as self-awareness and empathy, and their financial performance. Now, new research extends that base. Drawing on two years of research, the authors contend that the leader's mood and his or her attendant behaviors have enormous effects on bottom-line performance. Accordingly, top executives' primary task is emotional leadership. Therefore, leaders must first attend to the impact of their moods and behaviors. To help them do that, the authors introduce a five-step process of self-reflection and planning.

Daniel Goleman. "What Makes a Leader?" *Harvard Business Review* OnPoint Enhanced Edition. Boston: Harvard Business School Publishing, 2000.

Superb leaders have very different ways of directing a team, a division, or a company. Some are subdued and analytical; others are charismatic and go with their gut. And different situations call for different types of leadership. Most mergers need a sensitive negotiator at the helm, whereas many turnarounds require a more forceful kind of authority. The author has found, however, that effective leaders are alike in one crucial way: They all have a high degree of what has come to be known as emotional intelligence. The components of emotional intelligence—self-awareness, self-regulation, motivation, empathy, and social skill—can sound unbusinesslike. But exhibiting emotional intelligence in the workplace does not mean simply controlling your anger or getting along with people. Rather, it means understanding your own and other people's emotional makeup well enough to move people in the direction of accomplishing your company's goals.

Harvard Business School Publishing. "How to Lead When You're Not the Boss." *Harvard Management Update*, March 2000.

If you're like most managers, you regularly find yourself in situations where you have the responsibility but not the authority to get things done through a group. Negotiation experts Roger Fisher and Alan Sharp have developed a leadership model called "lateral leadership," which allows a person to lead a group regardless of his or her formal role. Their five-step method includes setting clear objectives, thinking systematically, learning from experience, and being able to engage the other participants and give them effective feedback.

Harvard Business School Publishing. "Trust: How to Build It, Earn It—and Reestablish It When It's Broken." *Harvard Management Update*, September 2000.

In earlier decades, it may have been enough simply to understand the link between trust and financial performance on a theoretical level. Today, however, the demands are greater: The connection must be made actionable, and managers must be able to deploy trust in ways that yield tangible results. But before you can be trusted, you have to be willing to trust others. Try too earnestly to foster it, and your efforts can backfire, instilling suspicion among employees. What follows is some concrete advice for dealing with trust, an admittedly squishy subject. Includes the sidebar "How to Heal from Betrayal" and a list of additional resources.

Ronald A. Heifetz and Loren Gary. "The Work of a Modern Leader: An Interview with Ron Heifetz." *Harvard Management Update*, April 1997.

This interview explores organizational and individual resistance to the work of adaptive leadership, examining Heifetz's principles of "getting on the balcony" and "regulating distress" in some detail.

Linda Hill and Loren Gary. "What You Must Learn to Become a Manager: An Interview with Linda Hill." *Harvard Management Update*, July 1997.

Professor Hill explains the psychological transition that newly minted managers undergo. Beyond the change in functions, new managers are forced to adopt a new identity and to alter how they measure success.

John P. Kotter. "What Leaders Really Do." *Harvard Business Review* OnPoint Enhanced Edition. Boston: Harvard Business School Publishing, 2000.

Leadership and management are two distinctive and complementary systems of action, each with its own function and characteristic activities. Management involves coping with complexity, while leadership involves coping with change. Most U.S. corporations actively seek out people with leadership potential and expose them to career experiences designed to develop that potential.

Jennifer McFarland. "Leading Quietly." *Harvard Management Update*, July 2001.

Leaders are not always rough-and-ready heroes; rather, those who practice "tempered radical[ism]" can stay both inside and outside the system, pushing the organization to see new ways of thinking and learning. Leaders need to listen to those around them, especially those who have new ideas, radical or not.

Noel Tichy and Tom Brown. "Companies Don't Develop Leaders, CEOs Do: An Interview with Noel Tichy." *Harvard Management Update*, October 1997.

Professor Tichy discusses the importance of the CEO's role in leadership development. He asserts that the best people in the company to educate and develop future leaders are those who have a record of success that others can learn from.

Linda Klebe Trevino, Laura Pincus Hartman, and Michael Brown. "Moral Person and Moral Manager: How Executives Develop a Reputation for Ethical Leadership." *California Management Review*, July 2000.

Based on interviews with senior executives and corporate ethics officers, this article reveals that a reputation for executive ethical leadership rests on two essential pillars: the executive's visibility as a moral person (based on perceived traits, behaviors, and decision-making processes) and visibility as a moral manager (based on role modeling, use of the reward system, and communication). The article also offers guidelines for cultivating a reputation for ethical leadership.

Margaret Wheatley and Walter Kiechel. "The Dance of Change in Corporate America: An Interview with Margaret Wheatley." *Harvard Management Update*, November 1996.

Wheatley discusses the struggle occurring within American corporations between traditional structures and self-organizing forms, in which networks, patterns, and structures emerge without external imposition or direction. The role of a leader in an organization is changing profoundly. While some leaders have become more thoughtful, others feel threatened by the changes. Wheatley argues that the preservation of personal power and status is antithetical to learning organizations.

Abraham Zaleznik. "Managers and Leaders: Are They Different?" *Harvard Business Review* OnPoint Enhanced Edition. Boston: Harvard Business School Publishing, 2001.

Managers tend to exercise their skills in diplomacy and focus on decision-making processes within an organization. They wish to create an ordered corporate structure and are emotionally detached from their work. Leaders, in contrast, direct their energies toward introducing new approaches and ideas. Leaders engender excitement through their work and often realize their potential through one-to-one relationships with mentors. Business organizations can foster the development of leaders by establishing such relationships between junior and senior executives. This article includes a retrospective commentary by the author.

Books

Marvin Bower. *Will to Lead: Running a Business with a Network of Leaders.* Boston: Harvard Business School Press, 1997.

Although the command-and-control style of leadership once contributed to the building of America's might, Bower argues it is no longer the best system for today's intensely competitive global marketplace. People down the line don't like the system and don't do their best work under it. Moreover, command-and-control management breeds rigidity and excessive reliance on authority. Bower urges companies to shift away from managing through authority and hierarchy to running a business with a network of leaders and leadership teams dispersed strategically throughout the business. He describes the factors in designing a leadership company and explains how leadership can be learned on the job.

Daniel Goleman, Richard Boyatzis, and Annie McKee. *Primal Leadership: Realizing the Power of Emotional Intelligence.* Boston: Harvard Business School Press, 2002.

Daniel Goleman's international best-seller *Emotional Intelligence* forever changed our concept of "being smart," proving that emotional intelligence (EI)—how we handle ourselves and our relationships—matters more than IQ. His next book, *Working with Emotional Intelligence,* proved that personal career success also depends primarily on EI. Now, Goleman teams with Richard Boyatzis and Annie McKee—experts on the cutting edge of EI research—to explore the consequences of emotional intelligence for leaders and organizations. Unveiling scientific evidence that links organizational success or failure to "primal leadership," the authors argue that a leader's emotions are contagious and must resonate enthusiasm if an organization is to thrive.

Kurt Hanks. *Motivating People: How to Motivate Others to Do What You Want* and *Thank You for the Opportunity*. Menlo Park, CA: Crisp Publications, 1991.

This easy-to-read book contains succinct and practical tips on what motivates people and plenty of do's and don'ts in a well-organized format.

Harvard Business School Publishing. *Choosing the Right Leadership Style: No Single Approach Fits All Situations. Harvard Business Review* OnPoint Collection. Boston: Harvard Business School Publishing, 2001.

This collection of OnPoint-enhanced articles from *Harvard Business Review* explores the connections between leadership and performance improvement without settling on a "one-size-fits-all" prescription.

Harvard Business School Publishing. *Harvard Business Review on Change*. Harvard Business Review Paperback Series. Boston: Harvard Business School Press, 1998.

The *Harvard Business Review* paperback series is designed to bring today's managers and professionals the fundamental information they need to stay competitive in a fast-moving world. Here are the landmark ideas that have established the *Harvard Business Review* as required reading for ambitious businesspeople in organizations around the globe. From the seminal article "Leading Change" by John Kotter to Paul Strebel on "Why Do Employees Resist Change?" this collection is the most comprehensive resource available for embracing corporate change—and using it to your company's greatest advantage.

Harvard Business School Publishing. *Harvard Business Review on Leadership. Harvard Business Review* Paperback Series. Boston: Harvard Business School Press, 1998.

This collection gathers together eight of the *Harvard Business Review*'s most influential articles on leadership, challenging many long-held assumptions about the true sources of power and authority.

Harvard Business School Publishing. *How to Keep Your Employees Motivated, Productive, and Loyal. Harvard Business Review* Collection. Boston: Harvard Business School Publishing, 1999.

The collection includes "An Uneasy Look at Performance Appraisal" (Douglas McGregor and Warren G. Bennis); "Pygmalion in Management" (J. Sterling Livingston), "The Set-Up-To-Fail Syndrome" (Jean-Francois Manzoni and Jean-Louis Barsoux), "One More Time: How Do You Motivate Employees?" (Frederick Herzberg), "The Power of Predictability" (Howard H. Stevenson and Mihnea C. Moldoveanu), and "Nobody Trusts the Boss Completely—Now What?" (Fernando Bartolomé).

Harvard Business School Publishing. *Motivating Others to Follow. Harvard Business Review* OnPoint Collection. Boston: Harvard Business School Publishing, 2000.

This *Harvard Business Review* OnPoint collection suggests that there are three factors in the motivational equation: the power dynamics between the manager and the managed, the emotional intelligence or maturity of the manager, and the manager's own definition of success.

Ronald A. Heifetz. *Leadership without Easy Answers.* Cambridge, MA: The Belknap Press of Harvard University Press, 1994.

In this acclaimed book, Heifetz lays out his innovative concepts of adaptive leadership by examining the leadership roles of Lyndon Johnson, Martin Luther King Jr., Mohandas Gandhi, and others. He explores their sophisticated techniques for creating holding environments, using conflict to provoke change, and giving work back to the people.

John P. Kotter. *Leading Change.* Boston: Harvard Business School Press, 1996.

The author examines the efforts of more than 100 companies to remake themselves into better competitors. He identifies the most common mistakes leaders and managers make in attempting to create change and offers an eight-step process for overcoming obstacles and carrying out a firm's agenda: establishing a greater sense of urgency, creating the guiding coalition, developing a vision and strategy, communicating the change vision, empowering others to act, creating short-term wins, consolidating gains and producing even more change, and institutionalizing new approaches in the future.

Morgan W. McCall, Jr. *High Flyers: Developing the Next Generation of Leaders.* Boston: Harvard Business School Press, 1997.

The author offers an alternative to the conventional view of executive development as a fairly systematic process of identifying the right competencies and then selecting the right individuals. In place of the competency approach, McCall proposes a developmental model for growing executive talent that places utmost importance on experience as the linchpin of development. The ability to learn from experience, coupled with exposure to appropriate experience, creates an opportunity to learn executive skills. He offers numerous recommendations and interventions that will improve the probability that people will actually learn from experience—and remain open to continuous learning and development throughout their careers.

Bob Nelson and Burton Morris. *1001 Ways to Energize Employees.* New York: Workman Publishing Company, 1996.

This wonderfully entertaining collection of real-life examples shows how creative leaders motivate others. It will inspire even the weariest manager with practical ideas that can be implemented quickly and simply.

Robert E. Staub II. *The Heart of Leadership: 12 Practices of Courageous Leaders.* Provo, UT: Executive Excellence Publishing, 1996.

This book offers a practical and thorough examination of 12 practices of effective leaders. Staub intersperses advice from top leaders with plenty of lists, comparisons, and how-to information.

David Ulrich, Jack Zenger, and Norman Smallwood. *Results-Based Leadership.* Boston: Harvard Business School Press, 1999.

A landmark book, *Results-Based Leadership* challenges the conventional wisdom surrounding leadership. Authors Ulrich, Zenger, and Smallwood—world-renowned experts in human resources and training—argue that it is not enough to gauge leaders by personal traits such as character, style, and values. Rather, effective leaders know how to connect these leadership attributes with results.

Gary Yukl. *Leadership in Organizations.* 5th ed. Upper Saddle River: NJ, Prentice Hall, 2002.

A comprehensive text on the theory and practice of leadership, including topics such as effective leadership behavior, power and influence, types of leadership, strategic leadership, team leadership, ethical issues, cross-cultural leadership, and managing diversity.

eLearning Products

Harvard Business School Publishing. *Influencing and Motivating Others*. Boston: Harvard Business School Publishing, 2001. Online program.

Have you ever noticed how some people seem to have a natural ability to stir people to action? *Influencing and Motivating Others* provides actionable lessons on getting better results from direct reports (influencing performance), greater cooperation from your peers (lateral leadership), and stronger support from your own boss and senior management (persuasion). Managers will learn the secrets of "lateral leadership" (leading peers), negotiation and persuasion skills, and how to distinguish between effective and ineffective motivation methods. Through interactive cases, expert guidance, and activities for immediate application at work, this program helps managers to assess their ability to effectively persuade others, measure motivation skills, and enhance employee performance.

Harvard Business School Publishing. *Leadership Transitions*. Boston: Harvard Business School Publishing, 2001. Online program.

Whether taking on a new position in your current company or starting in a new organization, *Leadership Transitions* will help you succeed. This performance support resource, built with the expertise of Michael Watkins, prepares managers with the knowledge they need when they need it. Managers will learn to diagnose situations, assess vulnerabilities, accelerate learning, prioritize to succeed, work with a new boss, build teams, create partnerships, and align units. The program consists of a wide array of assessments and planning tools that learners can use throughout a transition period.

Harvard Business School Publishing. *What Is a Leader?* Boston: Harvard Business School Publishing, 2001. Online program.

What Is a Leader? is the most tangible, relevant online leadership program available on the market today. You will actively and immediately apply concepts to help you grow from a competent manager to an exceptional leader. Use this program to assess your ability to lead your organization through fundamental change, evaluate your leadership skills by examining how you allocate your time, and analyze your emotional intelligence to determine your strengths and weaknesses as a leader. In addition, work through interactive, real-world scenarios to determine what approach to take when diagnosing problems, learn to manage and even use the stress associated with change, empower others, and practice empathy when managing the human side of interactions. Based on the research and writings of John Kotter, author of *Leading Change*, and other of today's top leadership experts, this program is essential study for anyone charged with setting the direction of—and providing the motivation for—a modern organization.

Sources for
Leading People

We would like to acknowledge the sources that aided in developing this topic.

Lloyd Baird, professor, School of Management, and faculty director, Leadership Institute, Boston University

Warren G. Bennis, professor of business administration, University of Southern California

Larry Bird, basketball player and coach, NBA

Loren Gary, editor, *Harvard Management Update*

Daniel Goleman, consultant and psychologist

Douglas T. Hall, director of the Executive Development Roundtable, Boston University

Rakesh Khurana, assistant professor of organizational behavior, Harvard Business School

Hara Estroff Marano, editor-at-large, *Psychology Today*

Gordon Sullivan, Chief of Staff, U.S. Army (retired)

Andrew Young, U.N. Ambassador; Mayor of Atlanta, Georgia; Civil Rights Leader

Gary Yukl, professor, School of Business, State University of New York at Albany

Notes

Notes

Notes

Notes

Notes

Notes

Notes

Notes

Notes

Notes

Notes

Notes

Notes

How to Order

Harvard Business School Press publications are available world-wide from your local bookseller or online retailer.

You can also call:
1-800-668-6780

Our product consultants are available to help you 8:00 a.m.—6:00 p.m., Monday–Friday, Eastern Time. Outside the U.S. and Canada, call: 617-783-7450.

Please call about special discounts for quantities greater than ten.

You can order online at:
www.HBSPress.org